49 Excuses for Not Doing Your Chores

Copyright © 2018, 2022 by James Warwood

Published by Curious Squirrel Press

All rights reserved

No part of this book may be used, stored or reproduced in any manner whatsoever without written permission from the author or publisher.

Book cover design by: James Warwood
Book interior design by: Mala Letra / Lic. Sara F. Salomon

ISBN: 9798835064113
ebook ISBN: B07F6C53MT

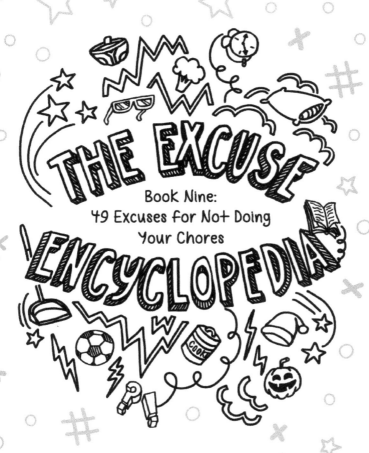

THE EXCUSE

**Book Nine:
49 Excuses for Not Doing
Your Chores**

ENCYCLOPEDIA

James Warwood

BOOK NINE

Excuses for Not Doing the Washing Up

CHORE EXCUSES

1. THE WASHING-UP LIQUID EXCUSE

We've run out of washing-up liquid . . .

. . . Why? Because we ran out of shower gel first. Which is more important: clean dishes or clean armpits?

2. THE DISPOSABLES EXCUSE

Ta-da! I've stockpiled on disposables . . .

. . . Disposable plates. Disposable forks. Disposable knives and cups and spoons and bowls and those little plastic things you find in motorway cafes you use to stir your hot drink. No one will ever have to do the washing up ever again!!!

3. THE FLAVOUR EXCUSE

You may call them *dirty dishes,* but I call them *flavoured dishes* . . .

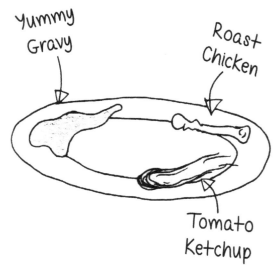

Yummy Gravy

Roast Chicken

Tomato Ketchup

. . . Think about it. You could be eating your dinner with the flavours of yesterday's roast chicken and the aromas of stone-cold homemade gravy with a hint of three-day old tomato ketchup.

4. THE YELLOW GLOVES EXCUSE

Hang on. You want me to wear these . . .

hideous yellow washing-up gloves

. . . Don't you know that yellow is not my colour? Let me know once you've found multicoloured washing-up gloves with galloping unicorns up the arms and rainbow tassels dangling off the sleeves and then I'll do the washing up.

5. THE DISHWASHER EXCUSE

Don't worry. I've discovered something that will do the washing-up while we all watch the TV . . .

. . . It's called a dishwasher. Simply load in your dirty dishes, hit the start button and in one hour the stains are replaced with sparkles. It's arriving tomorrow so let's leave the washing-up and go watch cartoons.

Excuses for Not Emptying the Kitchen Bin

6. THE DIGGER EXCUSE

Thanks to my digger we now have a bottomless bin . . .

. . . No need to worry about our garbage anymore. Our rubbish is China's problem now.

7. THE TRASH MONSTER EXCUSE

I've got a new Kitchen Bin . . .

. . . He's called Kevin. FYI, he bites.

8. THE SEA CAPTAIN EXCUSE

Ahoy there, matey . . .

. . . Did you know that in my spare time I am a Pirate Captain. The hull of my Pirate Ship will be made out of empty pop bottles. The cannons will be made out of used toilet rolls. The sails will be made out of lots and lots of empty crisp packets taped together. So let's all get drinking, pooping and munching!

9. THE BROTHER'S BEDROOM EXCUSE

Hope you don't mind but I've moved the kitchen bin . . .

. . . I know what you're going to say - it's no longer in the kitchen. But I hope you'll agree it's now in a much, much more satisfying location.

10. THE OVERFLOW EXCUSE

You know the fairy-tale called *Hansel and Gretel* . . .

. . . I'm not going to lure innocent children with a trail of sweets. I'm going to lure an unsuspecting bin man with a trail of rubbish, trap him in the house and tame him to become our very own kitchen bin man.

Excuses for Not Setting the Dinner Table

11. THE CHOPSTICKS EXCUSE

I've thrown away all our cutlery and replaced them with these . . .

. . . It's what Asian countries use to eat their dinner. I am yet to master the technique but what I can tell you is that they are very good for picking your nose.

12. THE OPEN WIDE EXCUSE

I've had an idea. I propose that from now on we no longer eat from plates . . .

. . . Instead we take it in turns to sit in front of this target and open our mouths really, really wide. Oh, and I recommend not wearing your favourite t-shirt.

13. THE WHIRLWIND EXCUSE

I already set the table. Oh no! . . .

. . . It must have been a hurricane, a really really tidy hurricane that who blew all the plates back into the cupboard and all the cutlery back into the drawer.

14. THE MONOPOLY EXCUSE

I'm changed and ready to be the banker. Oh dear! . . .

. . . I set the table ready to play Monopoly instead of setting the table for dinner. You really should be more specific when you say *'set the table'.*

15. THE INDIAN EXCUSE

As a family at dinner time, I think we should be more cultured . . .

. . . In India, people use their hands to tear off a strip of naan bread and use it to scoop up their food. So let's ditch the knife and fork and eat like Indians tonight.

Excuses for Not Cleaning the
Rabbit Hutch

16. THE LIFE SWAP EXCUSE

I'm doing a life swap . . .

. . . Floppy is going to go to school, do my homework and finish my chores while I sit here on this pile of hay and nibble a carrot.

17. THE POTTY TRAINING EXCUSE

Has anyone attempted to potty train a rabbit . . .

. . . The answer is yes, ME! It's a work in progress but I'm confident it can revolutionise rabbit hutch cleaning for children everywhere.

18. THE FRAGRANCE EXCUSE

My new rabbit fragrance is going to be the latest perfume fad . . .

. . . Floppy is helping me collect and ferment the ingredients: essence of hay, nibbled carrot and concentrated bunny wee wee. It's gonna be huge in New York!

19. THE MACHINE EXCUSE

I've developed a new state-of-the-art rabbit hutch cleaning machine . . .

. . . It's a work in progress but once fully tested I should be able to clean the hutch in five seconds and make us filthy rich.

20. THE HOUSE RABBIT EXCUSE

I've decided Floppy should be a house rabbit . . .

. . . Look at how much he loves the great indoors. Plus, you'll be able to clean up the rabbit poop at the same as hoovering the house.

Excuses for Getting Out of the
Weekly Food Shopping Trip

21. THE STILTS EXCUSE

I need to stay at home and practice stilt walking . . .

. . . That way next week I'll be able to reach anything you want from the top shelf. Curry paste, exotic dried fruits, luxury toilet roll. Nothing will be out of reach for me.

22. THE SHOPPING PARTNER EXCUSE

If you're looking for a shopping partner, Fido is your best choice . . .

. . . He can fetch on command, he doesn't answer back and if you take him down the sweetie aisle he won't stuff chocolate buttons down his pants.

23. THE LISTS EXCUSE

Shopping list? Don't worry I brought my own today . . .

. . . this list is for Christmas but I've got another for my birthday, another for my next birthday and another for when I become Prime Minster of the United Kingdom.

24. THE TROLLEY EXCUSE

I can't come shopping until I've got my shopping trolley driving licence . . .

. . . I've booked my Theory Test and I am having trolley driving lessons with a qualified instructor. I'm hoping to get my licence and be ready to join you on the weekly food shop in six to twelve months.

25. THE ACTION MAN EXCUSE

Here's the honest truth. You don't need me to help with the food shop . . .

. . . You just want the company. Here, take my action man instead. He'll protect you from soviet spies and listen to your boring gossip about the neighbours.

Excuses for Not Walking
the Dog

26. THE WALKING THE HUMAN EXCUSE

I think I've worked out a way to improve dog walking for everyone . . .

. . . Turn it around and the dog walks you. All you need is a wheelie chair, a strong leash and one extremely energetic dog.

27. THE TWO WORDS EXCUSE

I have two words for you. ROBOT DOG! . . .

. . . He doesn't need walking. He doesn't need feeding. He doesn't sleep so he'll always catch burglars. He never poos or whines or pees on the floor when he gets excited.

28. THE ULTIMATE FETCH EXCUSE

No need to take the dog for a walk anymore . . .

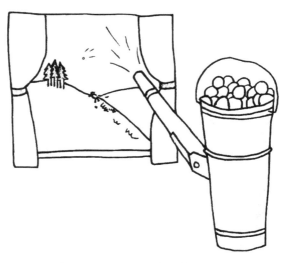

. . . This cannon will fire tennis balls a distance of 10,000 yards. I've got 100 tennis balls for the dog to go fetch. Fido is going to sleep well tonight!

29. THE FORGOTTEN EXCUSE

I can't walk the dog . . .

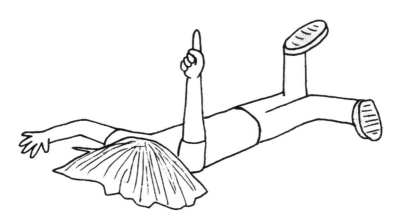

. . . Why? Because I've forgotten how to walk. Got a spare wheelchair?

30. THE GREAT OUTDOORS EXCUSE

The purpose of the dog walk is for the dog to poo outside . . .

. . . Well, I have the perfect solution. Let's all live outside! Embrace the great outdoors, become one with nature, poop in the bushes. The dog will be on a constant walk!

Excuses for Not Emptying the
Cat Litter Tray

31. THE THERAPY BATH EXCUSE

Did you know that cat poop is very good for your skin . . .

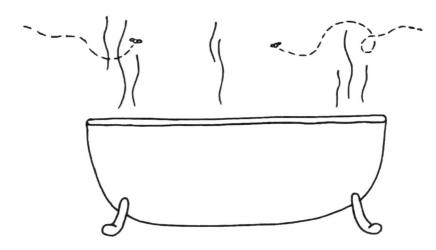

. . . That's why I've moved the Litter Tray to the bath tub so you can have a De-Wrinkling Cat Poop Therapy Bath. You'll need to wait a couple of months before there is enough to fully submerge your whole body.

32. THE NEIGHBOURS EXCUSE

Solved it! The cat can climb, right? . . .

. . . Good, because I've decided to move the litter tray. Now that it is on top of the neighbour's garage the litter tray is their problem now.

33. THE OPEN WINDOW EXCUSE

Nobody remembers to clean the litter tray . . .

. . . So I've taken it upon myself to train Felix to poop out the window. From now on everyone will need to remember to use this umbrella whenever you leave or enter the house.

34. THE CAT NAPPY EXCUSE

Why has no-one thought of this before? . . .

. . . I call it the Cat Nappy. Simply replace every night and no one will have to empty the Litter Tray ever again.

35. THE AGREEMENT EXCUSE

The cat and I have come to a mutual arrangement . . .

. . . I will ensure that her chin is scratched for 30 minutes a day and she'll always poop in the neighbour's garden. I hope you agree that this is a pretty good deal.

Excuses for Not Doing the Drying Up

36. THE TEA TOWEL EXCUSE

Ah, we've run out of tea towels . . .

. . . So, I tried to make some new ones from scratch. Could you pop to the shops and buy tea bags and paper towels. My first attempts were unsuccessful but I'm close to finding the perfect blend.

37. THE WET EXCUSE

How can I do the drying up? . . .

. . . I'm soaking wet. I'll never be able to make anything dry ever again! On the other hand, I'll be very helpful when the plants need watering or the dog bowl needs filling.

38. THE EMPLOYEE EXCUSE

I've hired some help to do the drying up . . .

. . . So far Nelly is yet to perfect the optimum blowing strength to dry the washing up. You are going to need to buy new plates, bowls, glasses, tea cups, side plates, coffee mugs, and those tiny little cups you drink espresso from.

39. THE WASHING LINE EXCUSE

I've had an epiphany . . .

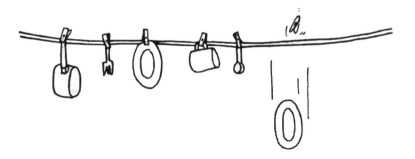

. . . We dry our clothes on the washing line, so maybe we should also dry the washing up here too. We can put our feet up and eat an ice cream while the sun does all the hard work for us.

40. THE UNDER THE SEA EXCUSE

Let's live under the sea . . .

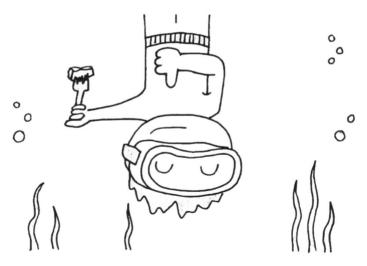

. . . No one would ever have to do the drying up ever again. Plus, I could make friends with a singing crab and go on an adventure to find a lost fish.

Excuses for Not Mowing the Lawn

41. THE JUNGLE EXCUSE

You said no to a pet monkey because we don't have a big enough house . . .

. . . So I'm cultivating a jungle habitat in the garden. I'm halfway there to a full jungle enclosure so do not bring any sharp objects near the foliage.

42. THE PROTECTED HABITAT EXCUSE

STOP! My name is Basil Von Licktonshoe and I am a Wildlife Preservation Officer . . .

. . . I have an official document to declare your garden as a Protected Habitat for Rare and Endangered Weeds. Never ask your child to mow the lawn or you'll be fined £100,000 and will be banned from all garden centres for life.

43. THE HAIRDRESSER EXCUSE

When I grow up I want to be a Hairdresser . . .

. . . Which means it's against my occupation to 'mow'. Instead I can 'snip', 'perm' or 'highlight' the lawn for a small fee while gossiping about B-List Celebrities.

44. THE WEATHER EXCUSE

I'd love to mow the lawn but first let's check the Weather Forecast . . .

THURS	FRI	SAT	SUN

. . . Oh dear. Can't do it in the rain as it's bad for the grass. Can't do it in a thunder storm as I could get struck by lightning. Can't do it in strong winds as it will ruin my hair do. Can't do it in the sunshine as I'll be in the paddling pool drinking ice cold lemonade.

45. THE BOWING EXCUSE

Are you sure you said 'mow the lawn' . . .

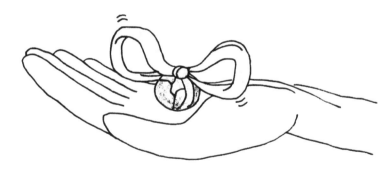

. . . I thought you said 'bow the corn'. Thought that was a strange request, but on the bright side I am now an expert at bowing small vegetables.

Excuses for Not Doing the Hoovering

46. THE SPIDER KINGDOM EXCUSE

I can't do the hoovering . . .

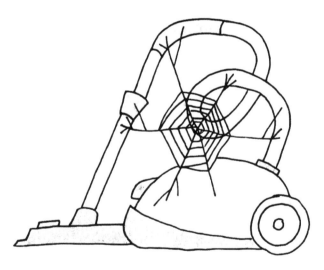

. . . Last week I hoovered up a massive spider. I fear that it has now made the vacuum it's Spider Kingdom, over which it holds full sovereignty.

47. THE ONE HOUR EXCUSE

Sorry I can't hoover until one hour after eating . . .

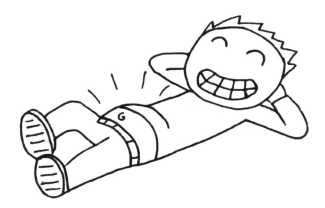

. . . That's right, it's very similar to swimming. The same applies to Maths homework and answering the question "How was your day?"

48. THE DEFLECTION EXCUSE

I want to do the hoovering, but I can't until my older sister has cleared the floor . . .

. . . And before she can clear the floor my older brother needs to do the dusting. And before he can do the dusting Dad needs to take us all out for an ice cream.

49. THE OLYMPIAN EXCUSE

Hoovering the stairs would disrupt my strict training regime . . .

. . . I will be entering the next Winter Olympics as a ski jumper and so I need the stairs to be as dusty as possible to simulate snow. I expect it will take at least 6 months of no hoovering to get to optimum skiing practice levels.

BONUS: IRONING EXCUSE

Sorry, I can't do the ironing . . .

. . . You see, I don't live in the Iron Age. I live in the Digital Age.

BONUS: 'RESET' THE TABLE EXCUSE

Oh, I seem to have misheard you . . .

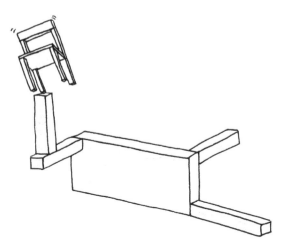

. . . I have 'reset' the table instead of 'set' the table. So our dining room table is now a piece of modern art.

BONUS: SAWDUST EVERYWHERE EXCUSE

I've found the perfect cleaning solution . . .

. . . Fill the entire house with sawdust. If you can't find the toilet, it doesn't matter. You can go anywhere you like, just like a rabbit.

BONUS: ONE CONDITION EXCUSE

I'll happily join you on the weekly food shop . . .

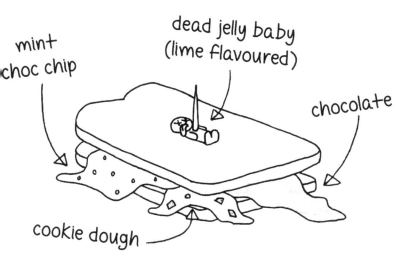

mint choc chip

dead jelly baby (lime flavoured)

chocolate

cookie dough

. . . but I have one condition. We have Ice Cream Sandwiches for dinner tonight.

BONUS: DOG PEN EXCUSE

No need to take the dog for a walk today . . .

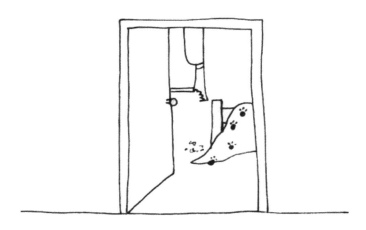

. . . he's in the new dog pen I've made. I admit that it didn't have to be in your bedroom, but you do have the most space and the nicest views.

BONUS: EVIL CAT EXCUSE

I think our cat is evil . . .

. . . He always looks like he is plotting something. Don't clean the litter tray! I'll go call the Bomb Squad just to be on the safe side.

BONUS: MISSING EARRING EXCUSE

WAIT! Mum says I shouldn't mow the lawn . . .

. . . She lost her earring when she was watering the plants this morning. You take the magnifying glass and I'll take the binoculars.

BONUS: FAIRY EXCUSE

No, I have not washed the dishes . . .

. . . but I have been dashing wishes. That's right, I'm a Fairy Wish Dasher.

BONUS: MOUSE ESCAPE EXCUSE

When I went to pick up my dirty laundry I discovered this . . .

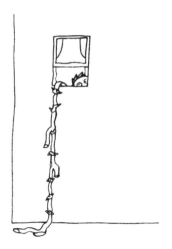

. . . As you can see, all my dirty laundry has been tied together and is hanging out of my bedroom. My pet mouse, Nibbles, has made a run for it.

BONUS: ECO-WARRIOR ESCAPE EXCUSE

I believe that cleaning is an act of violence against nature . . .

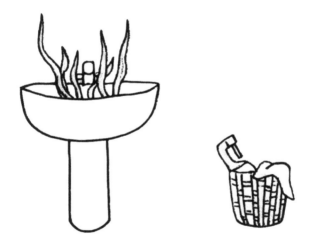

. . . Instead of attacking the natural world and our co-inhabitants, we should learn to live together in harmony. Join me and never clean anything ever again.

BONUS: DIZZY EXCUSE

I did start my chores . . .

. . . but then I began to feel dizzy. Can you see the stars and bird and lizard with a moustache flying around my head? Maybe I should go and sit down.

BONUS: BIG DISCOVERY EXCUSE

WAIT! I can't mop the kitchen floor . . .

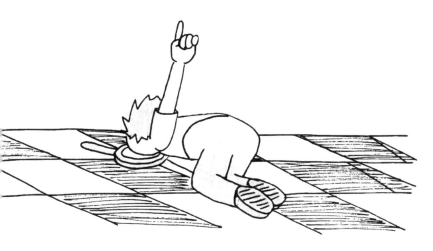

. . . I've made an important scientific discovery. I am not sure what it is yet but give me two to three weeks and I might win the Nobel Prize.

BONUS: SEAT WARMER EXCUSE

But I am doing my chores? . . .

. . . I am currently warming this seat ready for when mum comes home from work. I think that it is the most important task on my chores list.

BONUS: ULTRA VEGAN EXCUSE

Nope. I can't do my chores. Why? Because I am now an Ultra Vegan . . .

. . . I believe that humans should not kill any living thing, including bacteria with all of those nasty cleaning products. From now on I will be staying inside this circle so I don't accidentally squish any little innocent microbes.

BONUS: ONLINE CHORES EXCUSE

I can't do my chores now because I am doing my online chores . . .

. . . On my tablet, Sandy my online SIM, is currently cleaning the bathroom and then she needs to mow the lawn wash the car and cook the dinner. So, as you can see, I am far too busy.

BONUS: ICE SKATING EXCUSE

Maybe I shouldn't mop the floor today? . . .

. . . It's the coldest day of the year today, so if I mop the floor the water could turn the kitchen into an ice skating rink.

BONUS: NO HANDS EXCUSE

In order to do the washing up you need to have hands . . .

. . . But, due to accidentally chopping off my hands in a tragic nail clipping accident, I no longer have any hands.

BONUS: ARMY OF ANTS EXCUSE

Bad news. The dustpan and brush are broken . . .

. . . So, I've come up with an inventive solution to clean the kitchen floor. This is my army of ants. I'm going to shout orders at them while eating this sandwich.

ABOUT THE AUTHOR

James Warwood is a writer and illustrator who lives on the borders of North Wales with his wife, two sons, and cactus (called Steve the Cactus).

He has a degree in Theology, which at the time seemed like a great idea, until he released he didn't want to become an RE Teacher. Instead, he writes laugh-out-loud middle grade fiction and non-fiction. He also fills them with his silly cartoons. He is the bestselling author of the EXCUSE ENCYCLOPEDIA and the TRUTH OR POOP SERIES.

James likes whiskey, squirrels, reading silly books, playing his bass guitar, and Greggs Sausage Rolls. He does not like losing at board games or having to writing about himself in the third person.

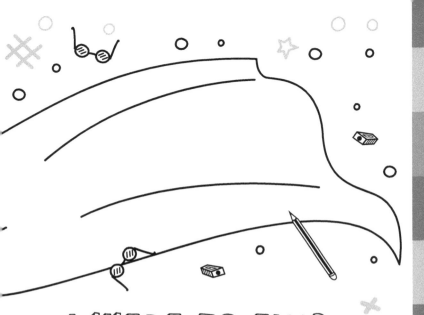

WHERE TO FIND JAMES ONLINE

Website: www.cjwarwood.com
Goodreads: James Warwood
Instagram: CJWarwood
Facebook: James Warwood

Want to join the
BOOKS & BISCUITS
CLUB?

Scan me to sign up
to the newsletter.

MIDDLE-GRADE STAND-ALONE FICTION

The Chef Who Cooked Up a Catastrophe
The Boy Who Stole One Million Socks
The Girl Who Vanquished the Dragon

TRUTH OR POOP SERIES

True or false quiz books.
Learn something new and laugh as you do it!

THE EXCUSE ENCYCLOPEDIA

11 more books to read!

GET THEM ALL IN THIS 12 IN 1 BUMPER EDITION!

820-page compendium of knowledge with 180 BONUS excuses

Scan me to activate your

25%
DISCOUNT